Chief

Who is in Charge?

illustrated by Toni Goffe

Child's Play (International) Ltd

Swindon   Bologna   New York

© M. Twinn 1993   ISBN 0-85953-782-X   Printed in Singapore

To Stephen
From Great Aunt Nora
Christmas 2017
Be a great chief!

Chiefs come in all shapes and sizes.
And in all sorts of uniforms.

Chiefs may look grand or fierce.   Even funny.

But what makes a Chief?
Would you like to be one?

Chiefs are strong!

Most of us avoid a fight.

People who want to be Chief
may go out of their way to find one!
The strongest and fiercest wins!

Chiefs need courage and determination, too.

We respect those who are stronger than we are.
In a violent world, we prefer a strong Chief.

Chiefs are ambitious.

The Chief of the tribe often wants to be Chief of Chiefs.

The trouble with warrior Chiefs is knowing when to stop!

If you don't, sooner or later you will meet your match.

Chiefs are often ruthless.

The more power ruthless Chiefs have, the more they want.

They think that they are special.
They behave like spoilt children.

They don't care how much
they make other people suffer.

Even the most powerful Chiefs don't live for ever.
They like to decide who will follow them.

If they can, they pass their rule on to their children
and establish an hereditary dynasty.

Divine right

Some Chiefs believe – or pretend –
that their power comes from heaven.
So, anything they do is right.
Anyone who opposes them must be wrong!
The people must obey.

Such Chiefs are often
very good actors.
They love to perform
ceremonies.

Chiefs may be wise, kind and good.

Not all Chiefs are mad, bad or dangerous.

But you won't become Chief,
just by being wise, kind and good.

If you are wise,
will you want to be Chief?

If you don't want to be Chief,
no one will force you.

People fear, obey, respect and trust even the worst rulers.

In our modern world, strong and ruthless dictators
still grasp power and surround themselves
with henchmen and secret police.

Why do people allow it to happen?
What can they do, if they are afraid to talk?

Yet, Chiefs only have power as long as the people allow.

When the people grow really angry, they unite,
overthrow their Chief and take back power.

Sadly, they give it away again just as easily.

There is usually another tyrant
waiting to step into the dictator's shoes.

What people want most is peace and opportunities for their children.

Dictators make fighting speeches about enemies abroad and at home and promise a glorious future.

Peace and prosperity, tolerance and education are the enemies of dictatorship. Gradually, nations become democratic. The majority decides. The people are in charge.

They elect their own representatives to make laws.

In a democracy, the people elect representatives to form the government. The majority decides. In some countries, the people choose the Chief directly. In others, the Chief is chosen by the government or the strongest party.

Chiefs of republics are often called presidents.
Usually, they are elected for a fixed term.
Some are just figureheads. Others decide policy.

Some democracies have kept their hereditary rulers.
They are born to be Chief and keep the job for life.

Over the centuries they have become gentler and nicer.

We expect all our Chiefs to set a good example.
That is no easier for them than for the rest of us and takes
a very strong sense of duty.   It is specially difficult
to be a good hereditary ruler.

Even in a democracy, ancient ceremonies are preserved and
past victories celebrated.   National pride lends strength,
but also contains the seeds of tyranny.

For
democracy to work,
there has to be a partnership
between Chief, government and the people,
A pyramid of power.   A strong and wise Chief at the top,
supported by a government elected by a majority of the people.

The people obey the law, pay taxes – and ask questions!
The government listens to the people.
The Chief listens to the government.
But, if one part fails,
fear, envy, pride, self-interest and
the wrong sort of Chief take over.
The pyramid collapses.
Back to dictatorship.
Or no chief at all:
anarchy.

In a democracy, most adults have the right to vote.
Practically every citizen has the right to become Chief.
Including you!

Do you have the will? Or a mission?
Do you have qualities of leadership?

It is hard to gain attention.
Can you persuade people to listen to you?
Do they share your views? Can you convince them?
Are you prepared to listen?
Are you ready to accept criticism as well as praise?

O.K. Then you are ready to start.

The odds are enormous.

India, the largest democracy, has 900 million citizens.
An Indian citizen has only about one chance in 70,000,000
of becoming Prime Minister.
A U.S. citizen has about one chance in 20,000,000
of becoming President.
A British or French citizen has about one chance in 4,000,000
of becoming Prime Minister, a Canadian one in 2,000,000 and
an Australian one in 1,500,000.

New Zealanders and Irish citizens are luckier.
They have about one chance in 250,000 of becoming Chief.

Is there anyone out there I can vote for?

Watch candidates for election performing on T.V.
Especially, those who want your vote.
Are they interested in you? Have you ever met them?
Do you know anyone who has? Have you tried?
Who do they really represent?

Do they have a message? What is it?
Do they just want power? Why?

Are they sincere? Are you convinced? Do you want to listen?

The freedom we enjoy was hard to win.   Don't let it slip away.
If we don't take part, the system will never work.
So, don't switch off!

We are more likely to vote for someone we admire,
believe in and share things in common with.
Perhaps, someone our own age.
Perhaps, someone who is not part of the system.
A rebel, like us! But maybe there is no one like us.

So, one of the problems in a democracy is
that the people who rule want to stay in charge.
They may represent not us, but themselves.
They may want power to serve their own self-interest.
They may not be like us at all and we may not like them.

Instead of voting for our local representative,
we may vote for the Chief we like or for an idea or party.
Not ideal, but better than not voting at all.

People often think that, apart from themselves,
society is corrupt. That is rarely true.
When one part is corrupt, usually, all parts are corrupt.

That makes it even more important to choose the right Chief.
Our Chief sets the standard for society and for us!
Our Chief has the opportunity to get things done,
perhaps to change the world.

What a shame, if we choose a Chief who does not have
something important to do! It is like a conductor of a great
orchestra, without a great work to perform.

To make it to the top is exhilarating!

As long as it lasts.

Power dissolves as quickly as it comes.
Ardent supporters melt away in a crisis.

All too often, Chiefs are surrounded
by colleagues who hunger for their job.

Sometimes, it doesn't seem so different
from the days of the old warrior chief.

Once in a while, a Chief arrives whose feet are firmly on the ground. Who commands respect, knows how to give orders, chooses able colleagues and works with them as a team

A Chief who knows what to do and puts service before self-interest.

A Chief who stays cool and can take a joke.
A Chief whose ear can be reached,
when the law and the authorities seem deaf.

Such a Chief is worth our support.

Press freedom is vital.

The media tell us what politicians are up to and let the Chief know what we think. They help to keep the lid on abuses of power. But the balance between a free press and autocratic government is very fine.

We get the press we deserve.
If all we want is scandal, the press will provide it.
The press is always ready to find fault, to make fun, exaggerate and even lie.

Don't believe everything you read.

The reason we need a Chief, even in a democracy, is to make decisions. Often, decisions none of us would like to face.

That is why it is so important, out of all the many thousands of eligible citizens, to choose a chief who listens, weighs the arguments and acts.

Chiefs have the best advisers in the world: scientists, soldiers, economists, judges, philosophers. They all think they are right. Most of them have something to gain.

Sometimes, advice can drive the Chief crazy.

Different types of Chief are needed in times of peace or war, prosperity or poverty.

Our Chief represents us and acts for all of us.
Sometimes, the Chief does what we want.
Sometimes, the Chief knows better than us what we need.
That's what makes a great leader!

In the end, the Chief alone may have to decide.
Being Chief can be lonely. And thankless.

Power changes people.
Some for better, some for worse.

GOOD CITIZENS
AWARD SCHEME

Good Chiefs don't act out of pride or vanity. They are humble. They respect the people they serve. They use their authority wisely and make decisions for the good of all.

Good Chiefs may overcome deep-rooted self-interest, prejudice and fear, and change the way people think.

Good Chiefs do not cling on to power. They prefer to lose it, rather than abandon their principles and beliefs.

By their example, good Chiefs bring out the best in us, too.

Followers make Chiefs.

As soon as we are old enough to vote, we have a democratic duty to choose the right people to represent us.

It is not always easy. We may like all the candidates, or none. We may feel they are looking over our shoulder.

But our vote is secret. Our business, nobody else's.

Suppose, one day, it is our turn. What will we say?

"My friends!
Let me be your Chief. I am one of you. We want the same things. I will represent and serve all of you.
I will listen to all points of view and respect
the rights and opinions of minority groups and individuals.

We will make good laws and change bad laws.
We will act together and combine our talents.
We will be thoughtful, honest, kind, fair, generous and
modest. We will help those in need.

I will set the standard. I will work hard. Follow me."

Isn't our Chief saying the same as us?

Once we have tried, we realize how difficult it is
to be Chief.   No Chief will ever please everybody.

You don't have to be Chief to set an example.
You can be a leader in whatever you do, by doing it well.
Each of us can set our own standard.
It is enough to be Chief in your own kitchen.

Good Chiefs and good citizens deserve each other.
In our democracy, we share responsibility.
We are all in charge.